WITHDRAWN

DIRTY AND DANGEROUS JOBS

Storm Chaser

By Joseph Gustaitis

Reading Consultant: Susan Nations, M.Ed.,
Author/Literacy Coach/Consultant in Literacy Development

WITHDRAWN

Marshall Cavendish
Benchmark
New York

Copyright © 2011 Marshall Cavendish Corporation

Published by Marshall Cavendish Benchmark
An imprint of Marshall Cavendish Corporation

All rights reserved.

No part of this publication may be reproduced, stored in a retrieval system or transmitted, in any form or by any means, electronic, mechanical, photocopying, recording, or otherwise, without the prior permission of the copyright owner. Request for permission should be addressed to the Publisher, Marshall Cavendish Corporation, 99 White Plains Road, Tarrytown, NY 10591.
Tel: (914) 332-8888, fax: (914) 332-1888.

Website: www.marshallcavendish.us

This publication represents the opinions and views of the author based on the author's personal experience, knowledge, and research. The information in this book serves as a general guide only. The author and publisher have used their best efforts in preparing this book and disclaim liability rising directly and indirectly from the use and application of this book.

Other Marshall Cavendish Offices:
Marshall Cavendish International (Asia) Private Limited, 1 New Industrial Road, Singapore 536196 • Marshall Cavendish International (Thailand) Co Ltd. 253 Asoke, 12th Flr, Sukhumvit 21 Road, Klongtoey Nua, Wattana, Bangkok 10110, Thailand • Marshall Cavendish (Malaysia) Sdn Bhd, Times Subang, Lot 46, Subang Hi-Tech Industrial Park, Batu Tiga, 40000 Shah Alam, Selangor Darul Ehsan, Malaysia

Marshall Cavendish is a trademark of Times Publishing Limited

All websites were available and accurate when this book was sent to press.

Library of Congress Cataloging-in-Publication Data
        Gustaitis, Joseph Alan, 1944-
           Storm chaser / by Joseph Gustaitis.
        p. cm. — (Dirty and dangerous jobs)
        Includes index.
        ISBN 978-1-60870-179-7
        1. Severe storms—Juvenile literature. 2. Thunderstorms—Juvenile
        literature. 3. Storm chasers—Juvenile literature. I. Title.
QC968.2.G87 2011
551.55023—dc22   2009049827

Developed for Marshall Cavendish Benchmark by RJF Publishing LLC (www.RJFpublishing.com)
Design: Westgraphix LLC/Tammy West
Photo Research: Edward A. Thomas
Map Illustrator: Stefan Chabluk
Index: Nila Glikin

Cover: Storm chasers study a powerful tornado in South Dakota.

The photographs in this book are used by permission and through the courtesy of: Cover: Visuals Unlimited, Inc.; 4, 6, 18, 22: AP Images; 9: © Eric Nguyen/Corbis; 10, 16: Getty Images; 11: © Bettmann/CORBIS; 12: © Reven T.C. Wurman/Alamy; 14: © Ryan K. McGinnis/Alamy; 15: iStockphoto; 21: Tinker Air Force Base History Office; 23, 28: R. Tanamachi; 25: © Gene Moore; 26: © Jim Reed/Jim Reed Photography - Severe & Unusual Weather/Corbis.

Printed in Malaysia (T).
135642

CONTENTS

1. **Facing Nature's Fury** 4

2. **Challenges and Dangers** 11

3. **The Thrill of the Chase** 16

4. **It Takes a Special Person.** 23

Glossary. 30

To Find Out More 31

Index 32

Words defined in the glossary are in **bold** type the first time they appear in the text.

Facing Nature's Fury

A scientist takes pictures of unusual twin funnel clouds in Kansas.

A tornado can be one of the scariest things in the world. People who have seen a tornado up close never forget it. A tornado is so frightening because it is so powerful. It can pick up an 18-wheel truck like a toy. It can rip trees out of the ground and send them flying through the air. It can peel pavement off a highway. A tornado can tear through a street of homes and leave them flat. Tornadoes kill about 90 people in the United States every year. They cause billions of dollars of property damage.

In the United States most tornadoes happen in an area called Tornado Alley. Tornado Alley is in the center of the country. It runs north from Texas and goes mostly across

FACING NATURE'S FURY

Oklahoma, Kansas, Nebraska, and Iowa. Tornadoes are also common, though, in many other states in the Midwest and the South. Tornadoes can happen at any time of year, but most happen in April, May, and June. Most tornadoes occur between 3 P.M. and 9 P.M., which is usually the hottest time of the day.

What Is a Tornado?

A tornado is a very powerful windstorm. It is sometimes called a twister. This is a good description because a tornado is a column of air that is turning, or twisting, very fast. A tornado is usually shaped like a cone or a funnel. It is wide at the top and narrow at the bottom. It is also very tall. The top of a tornado can be more than 10 miles (16 kilometers) high in the sky. The bottom of a tornado, where it touches the ground, is where the damage happens. The

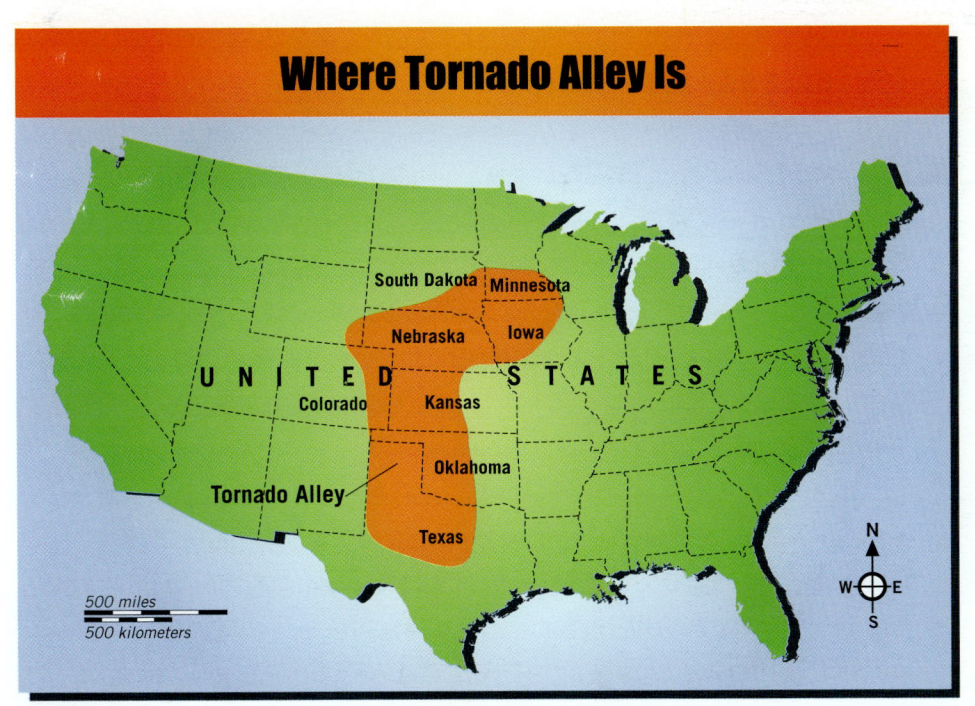

Where Tornado Alley Is

wind speed in a tornado may be more than 200 miles per hour (320 kilometers per hour). Because the wind is so strong, tornadoes can cause terrible damage.

Most people want to get as far away from a tornado as they can, as fast as they can. Some people, however, want to get closer to tornadoes. They wait until the afternoon sky gets as dark as night. The clouds turn an ugly green color. The rain comes down hard. The sound of the rain is so loud that one person can't hear another standing right nearby. That's when the people called storm chasers jump into their cars and head toward the storms.

Who the Storm Chasers Are

Who are the storm chasers? Some people chase tornadoes because it's their job. Most people who

Ted Fujita and the F Scale

Some tornadoes are more powerful than others. Scientists use something called the **Enhanced** F Scale to describe how powerful a tornado is. They give each tornado a number from EF0 to EF5. An EF0 tornado causes the least damage. An EF1 tornado causes more damage than an EF0. An EF2 tornado causes more damage than an EF1, and so on. EF5 tornadoes are the most destructive. They lift houses off their foundations and tear them to pieces. They rip the bark off trees. They carry cars the length of a football field. In an EF5 tornado, the **gusts** of wind are stronger than 200 miles per hour (320 kilometers per hour).

The Enhanced F Scale used today is based on an original F Scale that was invented by Tetsuya "Ted" Fujita of the University of Chicago in 1971. He was an **immigrant** from Japan. He had a special talent for understanding storms. By the time he died in 1998, he had become known as Mr. Tornado.

This storm in Oklahoma was an EF5 tornado, the most powerful kind.

chase tornadoes as a job are scientists. Most of these scientists are **meteorologists**. A meteorologist is a person who studies weather. Meteorologists go to school for years in order to become weather experts.

Meteorologists who study tornadoes want to learn more about them so they can better predict when and where these powerful storms will strike. If people have more warning that a tornado is likely to strike, they have more time to take shelter. That means they are more likely to survive a tornado unhurt.

To help make others safer, meteorologists who are storm chasers sometimes put themselves at risk. In cars or trucks full of special equipment to gather weather information, they drive to the area where the weather is worst.

Some other people who chase tornadoes as a job are photographers or filmmakers. They are able to sell dramatic pictures of tornadoes. Another kind of job for some storm chasers is taking people on storm-chasing tours.

A lot of people chase tornadoes as a hobby. For these people, storm chasing is fun and exciting. Sometimes, things these people see or information they gather helps scientists who study tornadoes.

There are many kinds of storm chasers. They all have their part to play.

Understanding Tornadoes

Tornadoes are usually caused by powerful thunderstorms, along with thunder, lightning, hard rain, and hail. The storm clouds that produce tornadoes are called **supercells**. In a supercell, warm air is pulled in at the bottom of the cloud. The warm air then rises up into the sky.

If the wind is blowing a certain way, the warm air starts spinning as it rises. If it spins fast enough, it takes on a funnel shape. That's when it's called a **funnel cloud**. Funnel clouds don't touch the ground, but they can still be dangerous. That's because of their high winds. When a funnel cloud does touch the ground, it becomes a tornado.

It's very hard to tell if a thunderstorm will create a tornado. Meteorologists, however, look for certain

Red Tornadoes?

Storm clouds are dark because of all the water in them. Tornadoes are dark for the same reason. Water is not all that's in tornadoes. They also pick up dust, tree branches, pieces of objects that are destroyed, and other things. Red tornadoes happen in some parts of the United States. They turn red because of the red dirt that they pick up. Red tornadoes occur mostly in Oklahoma and Kansas, where the soil is often red.

A supercell, like this one being watched by a scientist, is a type of storm cloud that may turn into a tornado.

signs. One sign is what is called a **wall cloud**. This is a cloud that drops down from a band of clouds and moves toward the ground.

When a tornado forms, it's almost impossible to tell exactly what path it will take. But the scientists who are storm chasers are learning more and more.

These scientists usually don't see a tornado doing damage. That's because they try to stay ahead of the storm, not behind it. That's not always easy because of the directions of the roads. But tornadoes usually are not very fast. Meteorologists estimate that most tornadoes travel at about 35 miles per hour (55 kilometers per hour). Storm chasers usually can drive faster than that.

Storm chasers often do see the destruction a tornado causes. One storm chaser who was a photographer saw a house that had nothing left but a bathtub, a toilet, and one wall. A neighbor told him that the family survived by "getting in the tub and covering up."

Meteorologist Howard B. Bluestein is one of the leading tornado experts in the United States. He has described how a tornado once picked up a cottage with two people in it. The storm carried the cottage through the air and dropped it in a lake. The people inside then swam to the shore.

The Tri-State Tornado

One of the most terrible tornadoes in U.S. history was the Tri-State Tornado of 1925. It cut a 219-mile (352-kilometer) path of destruction through the states of Missouri, Illinois, and Indiana.

It began near Ellington, Missouri, at around 1:00 P.M. on March 18. At least 11 people were killed in Missouri. At around 2:00 P.M. the tornado reached Illinois, where the worst damage was done. In the town of Gorham, most of the buildings were destroyed, and 37 people died. In Murphysboro, 234 people died. At a school in DeSoto, 33 children died. The tornado then moved into Indiana at around 4:00 P.M. In Griffin, Indiana, 150 homes were wrecked.

The tornado finally died out at around 4:30 in the afternoon. In all, the twister caused many millions of dollars worth of damage and killed almost 700 people.

The Tri-State Tornado destroyed many homes in the town of Griffin, Indiana.

2 Challenges and Dangers

This photo shows the tornado that hit Dallas, Texas, on April 2, 1957.

In the 1950s, many Americans began buying home movie cameras. **Amateur** photographers with home movie cameras took some of the first movies ever made of tornadoes.

One of the first tornadoes to be photographed by amateurs happened in Dallas, Texas, on April 2, 1957. More than a hundred photographers took pictures of the storm. Some of them took home movies. One of these home movies went to a meteorologist at the U.S. Weather Bureau. His name was Walter Hoecker. He studied the movie and was able to figure out the tornado's wind speed. It was 170 miles per hour (275 kilometers per hour). This was the first time that anyone had been able to estimate the wind speed of a tornado scientifically.

The First Storm Chasers

Meteorologists realized that photographs and movies could help them learn more about tornadoes. So, they thought, why not go out and look for tornadoes? The scientists became storm chasers.

A meteorologist named Neil Ward began chasing storms in the 1950s. Ward was a meteorologist with the U.S. Weather Bureau. Later he was a research scientist at the National Severe Storms Laboratory (NSSL), which studies powerful storms. When driving with his family on vacation, he would sometimes give them all a wild ride

Doppler on Wheels

In 1995, meteorologist Joshua Wurman invented Doppler on Wheels, or DOW. **Doppler radar** is a special type of radar that can show wind direction and speed. DOW is a Doppler radar system on the back of a truck.

DOW helped Wurman get better information about tornadoes than ever before. In 1999, Wurman and his team used a DOW device to measure a wind speed of 318 miles per hour (512 kilometers per hour) during a tornado. It is the highest wind speed ever recorded.

Doppler radar on the back of a truck helps scientists study tornadoes.

when he saw a storm and decided to chase it. In May 1961, he became the first scientist to take photos and movies of a tornado while on a storm chase. Ward became known as the "father" of storm chasers.

In 1972, meteorologists at the NSSL, which is in Norman, Oklahoma, started the Tornado Intercept Project, or TIP. Norman is in the heart of Tornado Alley, and TIP was one of the first organized efforts to find tornadoes in action and study them scientifically. In that same year, a group of meteorology students at the University of Oklahoma also began chasing storms.

The storm chasers didn't find a lot of tornadoes in their first year. But the weather got really wild in 1973. It was one of the stormiest years ever in the United States, with more than 1,100 tornadoes. The NSSL and the university chasers were able to find many tornadoes. One of the worst tornadoes they saw was a storm that wrecked Union City, Oklahoma, in August 1973. It was an EF4 tornado that killed two people. The scientists were unhappy to see all the damage. But there was also good news. It was the first time that meteorologists were able to watch the life cycle of a tornado from start to finish. They learned many things that allowed them to predict tornadoes much better. For example, they discovered that air starts spinning high in the sky before a tornado forms and touches the ground. They also learned that radar could help them tell that a tornado might be forming.

Keeping Safe

Storm chasers need to know how to stay safe. An important safety rule is: Don't get too close to a tornado. Usually, the best place to be in a car is a few miles ahead of the tornado. The chaser can see the storm, but the tornado isn't likely to get to the chaser's vehicle. A car can usually be driven faster than a tornado can move. Storm chasers try to avoid what is called **core punching**. Core punching is driving into the part of a thunderstorm that has the heaviest rain. In a very bad thunderstorm, a chaser's car can be hit by hailstones that are big enough to break the windshield.

The most dangerous thing about storm chasing is not the tornado. The biggest danger is driving in bad weather.

Getting Inside

Movie director Sean Casey has invented a special kind of truck called a Tornado Intercept Vehicle (TIV). Each one is built like a tank. TIVs are made to drive into a tornado. In June 2006, driving the first TIV in Texas, Casey saw a tornado ahead of him. The tornado came right at him. Heavy winds shook the TIV, and oil drums were flying through the air. But the TIV was not damaged, and Casey got some great movies. For the first time, someone had actually driven into a tornado and survived!

This photo shows Sean Casey in one of his Tornado Intercept Vehicles.

Storm chasers need to remember to get back in their cars or find other shelter if lightning approaches.

One risk is **hydroplaning**. That's what happens when water on the road causes a car's tires to slip. The driver can lose control and slide off the road—or even crash.

Sometimes animals walk onto country roads and highways. A driver chasing a storm has to be careful not to hit an animal. The driver also has to be careful not to lose control of the car trying to avoid hitting an animal. Lightning is a danger. Chasers who get out of their cars to set up cameras need to remember to take shelter if lightning gets too near.

If chasers get too close to a tornado, they are also in danger from all the material being blown in the wind. Tornadoes might carry tree branches, pieces of houses, and metal objects that are heavy or have sharp edges.

Fortunately, not many storm chasers have been hurt by lightning or flying objects, because they know how important it is to be careful. The risk is there, though.

3 The Thrill of the Chase

People on a storm-chasing tour in Nebraska watch for a tornado.

Storm chasing can be exciting. It can also be frustrating. A tornado is a moving target. When they're out driving, storm chasers have to make quick decisions about which road to take. One mistake and they can miss the tornado. Sometimes, they know where the tornado is, but there is no road to take them there.

So why do storm chasers do what they do? The answer depends on what kind of storm chaser the person is.

Tour Guides

The storm chasers who run companies that give tours of Tornado Alley want their customers to get their money's worth. These storm chasers take people who want to see a tornado on long drives through Tornado Alley in the springtime. The trips last for several days, and the visitors stay in motels. The people running the tours don't guarantee that visitors will see a tornado. People on a tour are likely to see tornado damage, though, and are almost certain to see some really strong thunderstorms.

Taking Pictures

The storm chasers who are professional photographers or filmmakers want to get the best pictures they can. Sean Casey, who invented the Tornado Intercept Vehicle, films tornadoes for IMAX and other movie companies. IMAX produces 3-D and other wide-screen movies that make you feel as if you are right in the action.

Another well-known photographer of storms is Mike Hollingshead. Working on his own, he goes on 40 or more chases a year, driving thousands of miles. It can be hard to make a living taking pictures of tornadoes. That's because the chasing season is short. Most tornadoes in the United

Storm Chasing for the Fun of It

Most storm chasers do it as a hobby. They love seeing the power of nature in action, and just about nothing is more amazing than a tornado. A lot of the fun comes from predicting where a tornado will happen. If you are a meteorologist, you might have a better chance of finding a tornado. That's because meteorologists have special training and equipment that's too expensive for almost any amateur to buy. But many storm chasers who are not scientists get very good at knowing where tornadoes will happen.

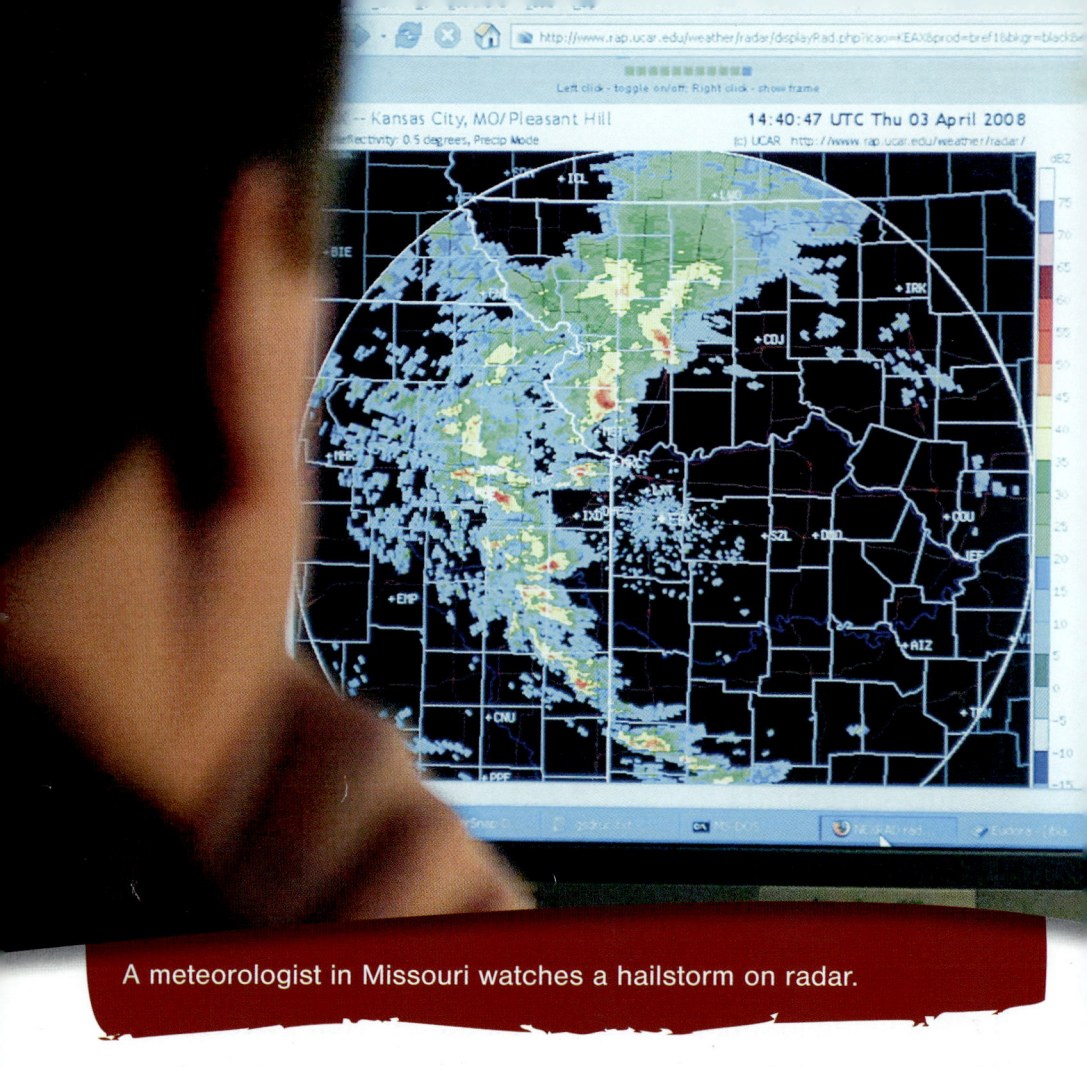

A meteorologist in Missouri watches a hailstorm on radar.

States happen in the spring. So a tornado photographer has to find something else to do the rest of the year.

The Scientists

Many storm chasers are scientists. They chase tornadoes in order to study them. They want to be able to better predict tornadoes before they form. If people can get more warning that a tornado will strike, lives can be saved.

Meteorologist storm chasers often work in special laboratories when they're not out driving. The laboratories get pictures of weather conditions taken from satellites. They collect weather information from a network of reporting stations all around the United States. They use powerful computers to analyze all the information they get.

Many of the scientists who are storm chasers work at the School of Meteorology at the University of Oklahoma. It is the largest meteorology school in the United States. The school is in the building in Norman, Oklahoma, that also houses the National Weather Center. At the National Weather Center, university and government scientists work together to study tornadoes and other types of storms. Tornado research is also done at the Center for Severe Weather Research in Boulder, Colorado.

When meteorologists try to predict a tornado, they look at many things. They get an idea of how **unstable** (likely to change quickly) the weather is. They study wind flow patterns and temperature. They use information they get from weather balloons, airplanes, satellites, radar, and weather stations. Weather balloons can give scientists information about how strong the wind is blowing high above the Earth. If radar tells the meteorologists that the air is beginning to spin within a supercell, they know that a tornado is likely.

No Forecasts Allowed

In the 1880s, a U.S. Army meteorologist named John Park Finley said that it might be possible to predict tornadoes. The U.S. government did not want tornado predictions to be made. In 1883, it said that meteorologists could not use the word tornado in any weather forecast. The government thought that using the word would make people panic. It wasn't until almost 70 years later that the government changed its mind because the science of predicting tornadoes had gotten better. In 1952, the U.S. Weather Bureau (now called the National Weather Service) was allowed to begin making tornado forecasts.

Another thing meteorologists look for is places where cold air is colliding with warm air. If one batch of air has a lot more water in it than the other, that's a sign that a tornado might form. Meteorologists use very powerful computers to create models of the atmosphere. These models help them understand the conditions that make tornadoes form.

When the conditions seem right for a tornado to form within the next few hours, meteorologists issue a **tornado watch**. When a severe storm is expected very soon or the storm is actually seen (or spotted on radar), they issue a **tornado warning**.

Warning Time

In 1986, the average time between a tornado warning and an actual tornado strike was about five minutes. That's not much time to get to shelter! Today, the average warning time is about 13 minutes. That's a difference of eight minutes—enough time for many more people to take cover.

The First Tornado Forecast

The first successful tornado forecast was made in 1948 by two meteorologists who were members of the U.S. Air Force. On March 20, a tornado hit Tinker Air Force Base in Oklahoma. Over the next few days, the two meteorologists studied the weather charts. On March 25, they saw that the weather looked a lot like it had on March 20. It was almost impossible that a place would be hit by two tornadoes in less than a week. But the weather looked scary. So they warned of another tornado. Three hours later, a tornado hit the air base. There was a lot of damage, but no one was hurt. One of the forecasters, Captain Robert C. Miller, later wrote that "we became instant heroes."

THE THRILL OF THE CHASE

Planes were pushed into each other and damaged by the tornado that hit Tinker Air Force Base on March 20, 1948.

STORM CHASER

In January 2008, meteorologists warned the people of Caledonia, Mississippi, 41 minutes before a tornado hit. Students in the school took shelter. That was lucky because a tornado hit the school. A school bus landed on the roof. Many lives may have been saved by the early warning.

The death toll from tornadoes has gone down a lot. Scientists say that better warnings are the reason. Scientists who are storm chasers have had a great deal to do with that improvement.

The tornado that hit Caledonia, Mississippi, in 2008 blew a bus onto the roof of this school.

4 It Takes a Special Person

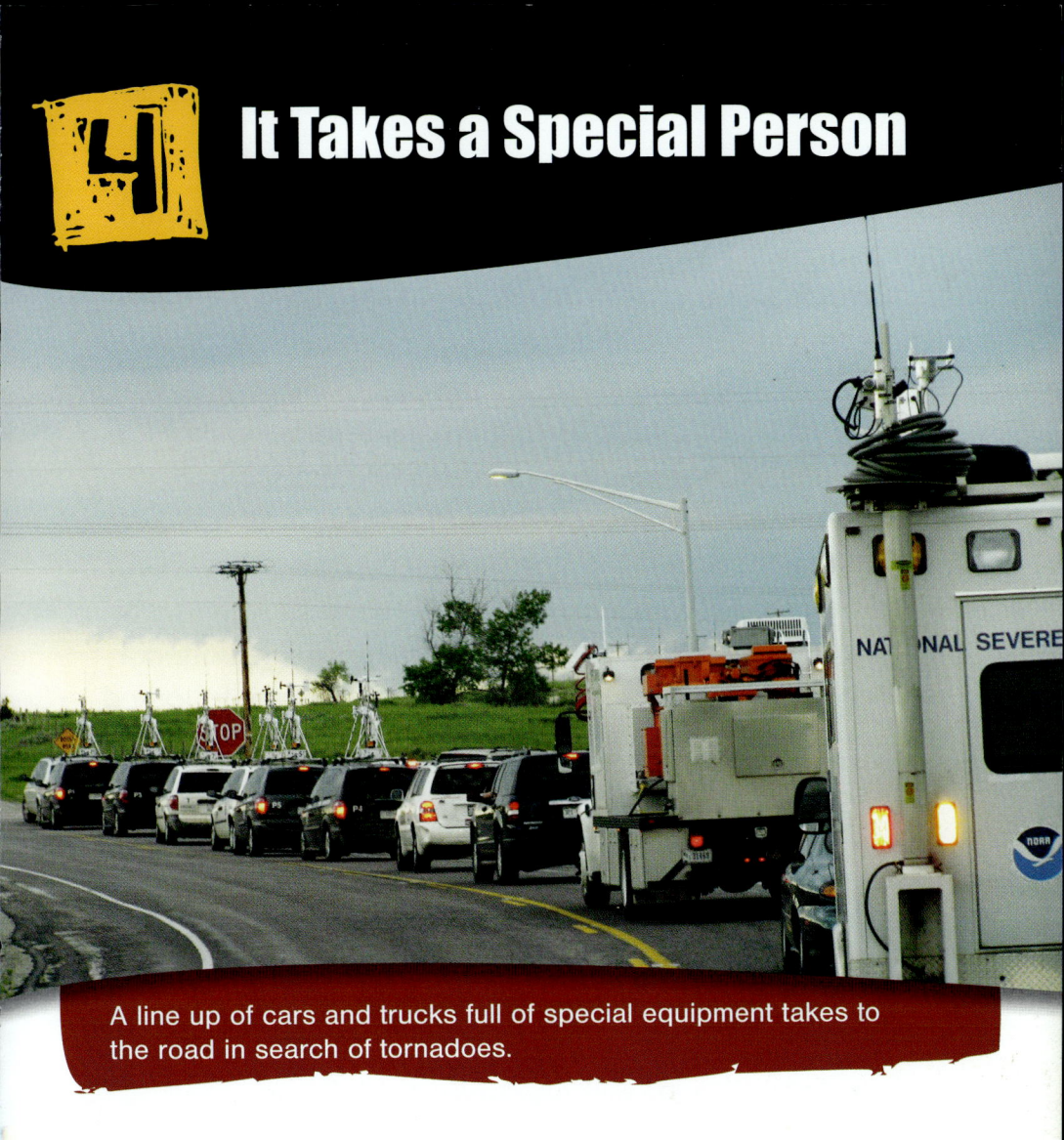

A line up of cars and trucks full of special equipment takes to the road in search of tornadoes.

One of the most difficult things about chasing tornadoes is actually finding one. It is still extremely hard to predict exactly where a tornado will strike. The area in which tornadoes might occur is huge. Even scientists with the latest equipment can spend days or weeks out in the field without finding one. Very few tornado chases end with the chasers being able to collect information about a powerful tornado. Both meteorologists and amateurs spend much of their time sitting in a car in bad weather, watching the sky. It can get boring. Sometimes the chasers stay out into the evening looking for storms. They may not get home until late at night.

On one storm chase, the chasers kept going to a spot where they thought tornadoes would be occurring only to find they had gone to the wrong place. First the storm chasers drove to Kansas. Then they heard there was a tornado in Oklahoma. They drove to Oklahoma, but a tornado then happened in Kansas.

The day on which the storm chasers were doing this was April 26, 1991. Meteorologist Howard Bluestein was leading the team of storm chasers. Finally, they spotted a really big tornado. It was ahead of them, so they followed it. They saw terrible destruction that the tornado had left behind. Telephone poles had been thrown half a mile (more than three-quarters of a kilometer). Later, they studied photos of the damage and the information their radar had recorded. They were able to figure out the tornado's wind speed. They had seen the rarest and most powerful of all tornadoes—an EF5! The storm became known as the famous Red Rock Tornado. It got that name because it touched down one mile (1.6 kilometers) away from the town of Red Rock, Oklahoma.

The Red Rock Tornado

Red Rock is a small town in northern Oklahoma. Only a few hundred people live there. The powerful tornado that touched down near the town in 1991 destroyed farm houses and other buildings. It took the bark off trees and lifted pavement off roads. Fortunately, very few people were hurt. The damage could have been much worse if the tornado had touched down in an area where many more people lived.

IT TAKES A SPECIAL PERSON

This powerful tornado caused terrible damage near the town of Red Rock, Oklahoma.

Cars Full of Equipment

The cars that meteorologists use carry a lot of equipment. They may have devices for measuring wind speed and air pressure. They may have lightning detectors that can find lightning almost 50 miles (80 kilometers) away. Some larger vehicles carry their own radar.

Cameras are a must. So are cell phones to keep in touch with the scientists back at the research center who might be able to help them find out where a tornado is likely to happen. A cell phone can also be used to call for help in case of an emergency.

Storm chaser Tim Samaras checks the radar in his car for signs of a tornado.

Good maps are important, too. Meteorologists use GPS (Global Positioning System) equipment. GPS devices link to satellites high above the Earth's surface. They let users know exactly where they are at all times. This helps them when they are on roads they don't know. Or if storm chasers hear on the radio that a tornado is occurring somewhere, the GPS equipment can help them find that spot.

Laptop computers or handheld devices may allow chasers to search the Internet for weather maps. Chasers also use their radios to listen to weather reports from a

IT TAKES A SPECIAL PERSON

special network of radio stations. This network is called NOAA Weather Radio, or NWR. It is operated by the U.S. government's National Oceanic and Atmospheric Administration.

How Many Storm Chasers?

About how many people are doing storm chasing today? No one knows for certain, and the answer partly depends on how you define a storm chaser. The number of people, both scientists and others, who spend a large amount of time each spring looking for and observing storms may be only about a hundred. If you count students, filmmakers, and others who sometimes chase storms, then the number may be more than a thousand. When a very severe thunderstorm pops up in Tornado Alley during May, the number of people who will get in their cars and crowd the roads watching for a tornado may be even larger.

SKYWARN

Many people who are interested in weather and storms join a special program. It's run by the National Weather Service (NWS), and it's called SKYWARN. Almost 290,000 volunteers are in SKYWARN. They act as severe-weather **spotters** and send reports of severe weather to the NWS. Their job is to identify and describe severe local storms.

People who want to join SKYWARN sign up at a local NWS office. They first take a free class about severe weather. The class lasts about two hours. The volunteers learn how storms develop and how to tell if a severe storm might be coming. They are also taught how to report information, and they learn the basics of storm safety.

So You Want to Be a Storm Chaser

If you want to be a scientist who chases storms, you will need to study meteorology. Meteorologists need at least a bachelor's degree, and many scientists who study weather have a **doctorate** in meteorology or a similar branch of science.

Some meteorology students get their first jobs by becoming **interns** at places where scientists study weather. An intern works for little or no pay in order to learn more about a certain career from experts in the field.

Meteorologists who want to be storm chasers need to learn how to use the special equipment chasers take with them. They also need to learn the safety rules for storm chasing. That's why meteorology students interested in storm chasing begin by going along on chases with their teachers.

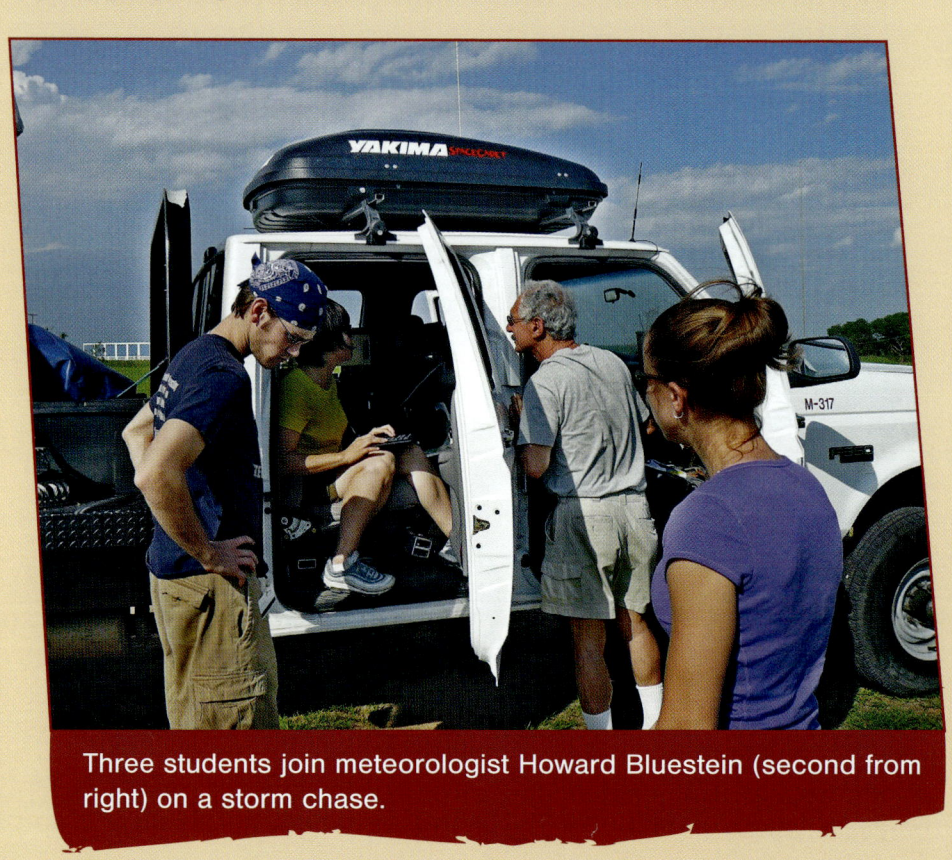

Three students join meteorologist Howard Bluestein (second from right) on a storm chase.

IT TAKES A SPECIAL PERSON

Some amateur storm chasers act as spotters. Spotters report what they see to weather officials. This can help scientists who are storm chasers get to the right place at the right time. Many people who are amateur storm chasers belong to the National Association of Storm Chasers and Spotters (NASCAS).

Twister

A lot of people found out about storm chasing when the movie *Twister* came out in 1996. It is a fictional story about storm chasers. It's an exciting movie with lots of action scenes. But most real storm chasers don't think the movie gives a very accurate picture of storm chasing. They think it shows storm chasers doing foolish and dangerous things, like trying to drive into the path of a tornado.

Still, many storm chasers were happy to see a movie that was about them. Millions of people who saw the movie found out about storm chasing for the first time. *Twister* made storm chasing seem important and exciting. After the movie came out, more people became interested in becoming meteorologists and doing storm chasing as their job.

Storm chasing may be a dangerous job, but a lot of people love it.

Storm Chasers on TV

A television series called *Storm Chasers* follows actual teams of chasers as they take to the roads of Tornado Alley in search of tornadoes. People watching the show can see some of the high-tech equipment chasers use, including Doppler radar and Sean Casey's Tornado Intercept Vehicles. They can watch chasers driving through stormy weather on muddy roads as they try to catch and learn about powerful tornadoes. Shown on the Discovery Channel, the series began its third season in the fall of 2009.

GLOSSARY

amateur: A person who does something for fun or as a hobby.

core punching: Driving a car or truck into the center of a thunderstorm.

doctorate: An advanced degree given by a university to someone who, after graduating from college, spends several years or more studying a certain subject.

Doppler radar: A special type of radar that can indicate wind direction and speed.

enhanced: Made better or stronger.

funnel cloud: A spinning column of air that does not touch the ground.

gust: A short, strong burst of wind.

hydroplaning: What happens when a car or truck slides out of control because there is so much water on a road that the tires cannot grip the road.

immigrant: A person who moves to a new country to live there.

intern: A person who takes a job for little or no pay in order to learn about a career.

meteorologist: A scientist who studies weather.

spotter: A person who watches for severe weather and reports what he or she sees to meteorologists.

supercell: A thunderstorm in which warm air rises upward and rotates.

tornado warning: A statement issued by the National Weather Service that says a tornado has been seen by people or on radar, or is likely to form very soon, and telling where it will likely hit.

tornado watch: A statement issued by the National Weather Service that says a tornado might occur within the next few hours.

unstable: Likely to change quickly.

wall cloud: A cloud that drops down from a band of clouds toward the ground. A wall cloud is a good sign that a tornado might be forming.

TO FIND OUT MORE

BOOKS

Hollingshead, Mike, and Eric Nguyen. *Adventures in Tornado Alley: The Storm Chasers*. New York: Thames & Hudson, 2008.

Lindop, Laurie. *Chasing Tornadoes*. Brookfield, CT: Twenty-First Century Books, 2003.

Reed, Jim. *Storm Chaser: A Photographer's Journey*. New York: Abrams, 2007.

Stanley, Ed. *Storm Chasers*. Parsippany, NJ: Celebration Press, 2006.

WEBSITES

http://www.chaseday.com
This website posts dramatic pictures for people interested in tornadoes.

http://dsc.discovery.com/tv/storm-chasers/storm-chasers.html
From the Discovery Channel, a website all about storm chasers.

http://www.livescience.com/tornadoes
The "All About Tornadoes" page of this website includes both information and pictures.

http://www.nssl.noaa.gov
This website of the National Severe Storms Laboratory includes a great deal of helpful information for students thinking about pursuing a degree in meteorology.

http://www.photolib.noaa.gov/nssl/tornado3.html
This website of the National Oceanic and Atmospheric Administration includes exciting photos of tornadoes.

http://www.spc.noaa.gov
This website of the Storm Prediction Center of the National Weather Service includes news and maps of storm activity.

http://www.weather.gov/skywarn
This website provides information about the SKYWARN program and about how volunteers can join it.

INDEX

Page numbers in **bold** type are for photos, maps, and illustrations.

amateur storm chasers, 11, 17, 23, 29

Bluestein, Howard B., 10, 24, **28**

Caledonia, Mississippi, 22, **22**
cars and equipment, **12**, 14, **14**, 15, 19, 20, **23**, 25–27, **26**
Casey, Sean, 14, **14**, 17, 29
causes of tornadoes, 8, 20
characteristics of tornadoes, 5–6, 9
core punching, 14
destruction and death, 4, 6, 9, 10, **10**, 21, **22**, 24
Doppler on Wheels (DOW), 12, **12**

Enhanced F Scale, 6

Fujita, Tetsuya "Ted," 6
funnel clouds, **4**, 5, 8

Hollingshead, Mike, 17
hydroplaning, 15

Illinois, 10
Indiana, 10, **10**
Iowa, 5, **5**

jobs and careers, 6–8, 28, **28**

Kansas, **4**, 5, **5**, 8

lightning, 15, **15**, 25

meteorology and meteorologists, **4**, 6, 7, 9, **18**, 18–20, 28
Missouri, 10

National Severe Storms Laboratory (NSSL), 12–13
National Weather Center, 19
National Weather Service (NWS), 19, 27

Nebraska, 5, **5**, **16**
NOAA Weather Radio (NWR), 27

Oklahoma, 5, **5**, 7, 8, 13, 19, 20, **21**

photographers and filmmakers, **4**, 7–8, 11, **16**, 17, 18
prediction and warning, 7, 13, 17, 18, 19–20, 22, 24

radars, 12, **18**, 19, 25, **26**
rain and hail, 6, 14, **18**
Red Rock Tornado, 24, **25**
red tornadoes, 8

safety, 7, 13–15
Samaras, Tim, **26**
satellites, 18, 19, 26
SKYWARN, 27
spotters, 27, 29
Storm Chasers (TV series), 29
supercells, 8, **9**, 19

Texas, 4, **5**, 11, **11**
thunderstorms, 8, 14, 27
Tinker Air Force Base, Oklahoma, 20, **21**
Tornado Alley, 4, 5, **5**, 16, 17, 27
Tornado Intercept Vehicle (TIV), 14, **14**, 29
tour guides, 8, 16–17
Tri-State Tornado, 10, **10**
Twister (movie), 29

U.S. Weather Bureau, 11, 12

wall clouds, 9
Ward, Neil, 12, 13
wind speed, 6, 11, 12
Wurman, Joshua, 12

About the Author Joseph Gustaitis is a freelance writer and editor living in Chicago. He is the author of many articles in the popular history field. After working as an editor at *Collier's Year Book*, he became the humanities editor for *Collier's Encyclopedia*. He has also worked in television and won an Emmy Award for writing for ABC-TV's *FYI* program. He is the author of *Chinese Americans* in Marshall Cavendish Benchmark's *New Americans* series and of the book *Arctic Trucker* in the *Dirty and Dangerous Jobs* series.